D1002077

JANE AUSTEN

JANE AUSTEN

A Critical Bibliography

BY

R. W. CHAPMAN

SECOND EDITION

OXFORD
AT THE CLARENDON PRESS
1955

Oxford University Press, Amen House, London E.C. 4

GLASGOW NEW YORK TORONTO MELBOURNE WELLINGTON
BOMBAY CALCUTTA MADRAS KARACHI CAPE TOWN IBADAN

Geoffrey Cumberlege, Publisher to the University

PR
4037
C5

FIRST PUBLISHED 1953
SECOND EDITION, REPRINTED LITHOGRAPHICALLY IN GREAT BRITAIN
AT THE UNIVERSITY PRESS, OXFORD
FROM CORRECTED SHEETS OF THE FIRST EDITION
1955

PREFACE

THIS compilation is addressed to Austenians in general rather than to the fastidious collector, who is already provided for, on the grand scale, by Dr. Geoffrey Keynes's *Bibliography* of 1929, with its wealth of detail and its precise facsimiles. I have not aimed at the completeness achieved, up to 1938, by the *Cambridge Bibliography of English Literature*.[1] Thus while I have included all the editions of the novels before 1890 as indicating the extent of their popularity at home and abroad, I have ignored the very numerous later reprints (except as they may include introductions of interest), since they are textually negligible and have no commentaries, unless the fanciful illustrations with which some of them are embellished or deformed may be so regarded. The bulk, on the other hand, of criticism and exegesis that has appeared in this century, largely in reviews or articles, is substantial. I have confined my attention to what seemed to deserve record.

I am in debt to many friends; especially to Dr. Geoffrey Keynes for condonation, and for advice and help to Mr. Beecher Hogan, Miss Mary Lascelles, Mr. and Mrs. Geoffrey Tillotson. Mr. Sutherland of the Taylorian Institution made the list of modern translations much less imperfect than it would otherwise have been.

R. W. C.

[1] The main part of this article is described as revised by myself. In fact I had discarded much that seemed of small importance; this was added by another hand—the actual 'reviser's'. The design of the *CBEL* excludes all comment that is merely occasional. Yet of the criticisms of Jane Austen the obiter scripta of Scott, Coleridge, Tennyson, and Charlotte Brontë are, as they deserve to be, among the most familiar.

163614

NOTE

A FEW corrections have been made in this second edition, and the ADDENDA, p. 57, have been enlarged.

R. W. C.

June 1954

CONTENTS

AUTHORITIES

GEOFFREY KEYNES, *Jane Austen: a Bibliography*. Nonesuch Press, 1929.

Cambridge Bibliography of English Literature. Edited by F. W. BATESON. Cambridge Univ. Press, 1940, iii. 381–4.

This list, which within certain limits aimed at completeness, was largely compiled by R. W. C. The section on early reviews was contributed by C. BEECHER HOGAN. The latest entry is dated 1938.

Jane Austen's Letters. My edition (1932, second edition 1952) lists in Index VI all references to the novels. The index of literary allusions in Vol. V of my edition of the novels comprehends (in the current issue) all the minor works.

See also Nos. 81 (the authoritative *Memoir*), 120 (the *Life* by members of J. A.'s family) and 169 (my own *Facts and Problems*. Many of my references to this last are to its index, where fuller references may be found).

I (1)

THE SIX NOVELS
1811–18

SENSE AND SENSIBILITY

1. 1811. Sense and Sensibility: A Novel. In three volumes. By a Lady. London: Printed for the author, by C. Roworth, Bell-yard, Temple-bar, and published by T. Egerton, White-hall. 1811. 12°. Each volume has a half-title.

Keynes 1. *Letters*, Index VI. For the relation of *S. and S.* to the early (before 1797) *Elinor and Marianne*, see e.g. *Facts and Problems* 219. See also 40 (J. E. Austen), 125 (Moore), 149 (Cecil), 159 (M. Wilson).

2. 1813. Sense and Sensibility: A Novel. In three volumes. By the Author of 'Pride and Prejudice'. The Second Edition. London [&c., as 1811]. 1813. 12°.

Keynes 2. *Letters*, Index VI. For changes due to the author see my edition, or *Facts and Problems* 219 (but my comment on the disappear-ance of 'a natural son', p. 119, is erroneous).

PRIDE AND PREJUDICE

3. 1813. Pride and Prejudice: A Novel. In three volumes. By the Author of 'Sense and Sensibility'. London: Printed for T. Egerton, Military Library, Whitehall, 1813. 12°. Each volume has a half-title.

Keynes 3. *Letters*, Index VI. For the relation of *P. and P.* to the earlier (1796–7) *First Impressions*, see e.g. *Facts and Problems* 219. See also 54 (Trollope), 137 (Muir), 139 (R. W. C.), 156 (Bowen), 166 (Kliger).

4. 1813. Pride and Prejudice: A Novel. In three volumes. By the Author of 'Sense and Sensibility'. Second Edition. London [&c., as first edition]. 12°.

Keynes 4. *Letters*, Index VI. My conjecture, in my edition of the novels, that J. A. made no changes in this or the third edition, was confirmed by the publication of Letter 74.1, from which we know that the copyright was sold to Egerton in 1812. There is no reason to suppose that he consulted the author before reprinting.

5. 1817. Pride and Prejudice: A Novel. In two volumes. [&c., as 1813]. Third Edition [&c., as 1813]. 1817.

Keynes 5.

MANSFIELD PARK

6. Mansfield Park: A Novel. In three volumes. By the Author of 'Sense and Sensibility', and 'Pride and Prejudice'. London: Printed for T. Egerton, Military Library, Whitehall. 1814. 12°. Each volume has a half-title.

Keynes 6. *Letters*, Index VI, and for 'intelligence from Henry' about Northamptonshire, Letter 78.1 (not included in the first edition of my *Letters*). *Facts and Problems* 220. For 'Opinions' collected by J. A. see 33. See also 43 (J. E. Austen), 123 (Farrer), 138 (Lascelles).

7. 1816. Mansfield Park: A Novel. In three volumes. By the Author of 'Pride and Prejudice'. Second Edition. London: Printed for J. Murray, Albemarle Street. 1816. 12°. Each volume has a half-title.

Keynes 7. *Letters*, Index VI. For changes due to the author see my edition or *Facts and Problems* 220. Note the disappearance of *S. and S.* from the title-page.

EMMA

8. 1816. Emma: A Novel. In three volumes. By the Author of 'Pride and Prejudice', &c. &c. London: Printed for John Murray. 1816. 12°. The book is dedicated to the Prince Regent, and the first section, of 2 leaves, contains only the title and dedication, the half-title being printed as P6, but intended for transference by the binder. The other volumes have half-titles in the usual place.

Keynes 8. *Letters*, Index VI. *Facts and Problems* 220. For 'Opinions' collected by J. A. see 33. See also 46 (Scott), 57 (Newman), 123 (Farrer), 127 (R. W. C.), 168 (F. R. Leavis).

NORTHANGER ABBEY AND PERSUASION

9. 1818. Northanger Abbey: and Persuasion. By the Author of 'Pride and Prejudice', 'Mansfield Park', &c. With a Biographical Notice of the Author. In Four Volumes. London: John Murray, Albemarle Street. 1818. 12°. There are five half-titles, preceding the Biographical Notice and the texts. An Advertisement by the Authoress [1816] records that *N.A.* was 'finished' in 1803.

Keynes 9. *Letters*, Index VI. *Facts and Problems* 219, 220, where the evidence is collected for the relation of *N.A.* to the book written in 1797–8 and to the book advertised (as *Susan*) for publication in 1803, and prepared for publication in 1816. Both novels were published posthumously. For Henry Austen's Biographical Notice see 47. For the cancelled chapter of *Persuasion*, the only scrap of the manuscripts of the six novels that has survived, see 29. See also 48 (Whately), 142 (Sadleir), 145 (Reid).

10. An interesting set of the first editions was described (by the late Greville Worthington and others) in Elkin Mathews's catalogues 70 (1937) and 88 (1946). These bear the signatures of

Cassandra Austen and of 'Emma Austen' (earlier, therefore, than 1837, when E. A., wife of J. E. A.-L., J. A.'s nephew, had become Austen-Leigh). These copies contain corrections that are clearly authentic; the most notable is in *P. and P.* ch. 6, where in 1813 and all editions Charlotte Lucas is made to say that married people, however like each other in the beginning, 'always continue to grow sufficiently unlike afterwards to have their share of vexation'. The correction is *contrive*, an obvious improvement (the corruption has been noticed elsewhere). In *N.A.* ch. 26, 'the chaise-and-four conveyed the two from the Abbey', the correction is *three*; this is right in substance; but J. A. no doubt wrote *trio*, easily misread *two*.

In the margin opposite the page of *P.* containing the words 'How eloquent could Anne Elliot have been,—how eloquent, at least, were her wishes on the side of early warm attachment' (and early, adventurous marriage) someone—surely Cassandra—has written: 'Dear Dear Jane! This deserves to be written in letters of gold.'

This set is now the property of Mr. J. Links.

FIRST AMERICAN EDITIONS

11. 1832–3. For the editions, published by Carey & Lea of Philadelphia, of *Elizabeth Bennet; or, Pride and Prejudice*, *Mansfield Park*, *Persuasion* (all 1832), *Emma*, *Sense and Sensibility*, *Northanger Abbey* (all 1833), see Keynes 10–15.
11*a.* 1816 (not in Keynes). *Emma*. Philadelphia, 1816.

I (2)

LATER EDITIONS

AFTER the posthumous publication of *N.A. and P.* in 1818 there was no printing until 1833. But even if the publishers' stock was exhausted, the book-clubs and libraries kept the novels in circulation. From 1833 Bentley's collected edition, and some separate editions, made the novels accessible until in 1892 a fresh impulse was given by Dent's attractive edition, which was followed by many more.

In 1815 Henry Austen declined an offer from John Murray of £450 for the copyright of the three novels that remained in the author's control. Murray accordingly published *E.*, and the second edition of *M.P.*, on a profit-sharing agreement. (*Life* 310, *Facts and Problems* 155). In 1832 Henry and Cassandra accepted Richard Bentley's offer of £250 for the five novels in their control, referring him to Egerton's executors for *P. and P.*

12. For Bentley's editions, virtually a part of his *Standard Novels*, of *Novels by Miss Jane Austen. Complete in five volumes*, 1833, 1837, 1866, 1869, 1878–9, 1882, 1886, see Keynes 27–32. In 1879 a sixth volume was added, reprinting the *Memoir* 1871. An appearance of uniformity with the other volumes was given by the lettering on the spine: Lady Susan &c. Jane Austen.

13. For separate editions (before 1890), other than Bentley's own in *Standard Novels*, see Keynes. See also p. 57.

S. and S.: 1844, 1852, 1857 (New York, with *P.*), 1864 (Tauchnitz), 1870, 1877, 1883, 1884, 1887. *P. and P.*: 1844, 1848 (Boston), 1852, 1857 (New York, with *N.A.*), 1870 (Tauchnitz), 1870 (Chapman & Hall), 1877, 1883, 1884, 1886. *M.P.*: 1846 (Belfast), 1851, 1857 (Routledge), 1857 (New York), 1867 (Tauchnitz), 1870, 1875, 1877, 1883. *E.*: 1849, 1857 (Routledge), 1857 (New York), 1870, 1877 (Routledge), 1877 (Tauchnitz), 1881, 1883. *N.A. and P.* 1850, 1857 (2), 1870, 1871 (Tauchnitz), 1877, 1883.

14. 1892. Jane Austen's Novels in ten volumes. Edited by Richard Brimley Johnson. Illustrations by William Cubit Cooke . . . Dent, 1892.

This attractive edition with its pleasing illustrations did much to make J. A. better known. The value of its 'editing' may be gauged by the editor's statement (in his 'Hampshire' edition of 1902) that 'there are no intentional variations in *text* between the different editions'. (See above, 2, 7.)

15. 1895–7. The Novels, with introductions by Austin Dobson and illustrations by Hugh Thomson and (for *P. and P.*) C. E. Brock. Macmillan 1895–7.

16. 1899. The Temple edition of the novels, illustrated by C. E. Brock. Dent, 1899.

These were not strictly collected editions, but for bibliographical purposes may be so reckoned. The illustrations, especially Thomson's, were very popular and still find admirers.

17. 1912. *Pride and Prejudice* 1912, edited by Katharine M. Metcalfe. Oxford.

This unassuming edition is equipped with a perceptive introduction and notes, and anticipates the textual rigours of the next item.

18. 1923. The Novels of Jane Austen. The Text based on Collation of the Early Editions by R. W. Chapman. Oxford 1923. 5 vols. 8°. Large-paper edition, limited to 1,000 sets.

This was the first attempt to establish the text by examination of all the editions in which J. A. had a hand and by admission, or record, of a few probable or plausible emendations. The moral of *M.P.* is illuminated by the addition of *Lovers' Vows*, and the cancelled chapter of *P.* is added from the *Memoir* (see below, 29). The notes give the textual variants between the editions, and attempt to explain obscurities and allusions. The indexes include real persons and characters, real and feigned places, and ('Literary Allusions') collect the evidence of the novels, letters, and minor works (as far as was possible in 1923) for J. A.'s knowledge of books. The numerous illustrations are all from contemporary sources. They include fashion-plates intended to suggest the dress of some of the heroines (in *S. and S.* I assume the costume of 1797 not 1811); views of London, Derbyshire, Brighton, Portsmouth, Box Hill, Bath, and Lyme Regis; in *M.P.* a view of a Northamptonshire house from Repton's *Landscape Gardening* 1816, in which he indicated his proposed 'improvement' by the device of a movable slip; in *E.*, Jane Fairfax's instrument by Broadwood, 1816, &c., &c.

Additions and Corrections 1925, a small pamphlet, 25 copies.

1926+. The edition was reprinted from the plates of 1923, on smaller paper, and with some minor corrections, in 1926 and later. The reprint of 1952 corrects some errors in the 1871 text of the cancelled chapter of *P.* The frontispieces were no longer in chromo-collotype.

I permit myself a reference to a flattering review of this edition by Mr. E. M. Forster (131).

I (3)

TRANSLATIONS

19.   FRENCH

1815 Raison et Sensibilité, ou les Deux Manières d'Aimer, traduit librement de l'anglais, par Mme Isabelle de Montolieu. A Paris . . . 1815. 4 vols. 12°.

1828. Raison et Sensibilité, ou les Deux Manières d'Aimer. Traduit librement de l'anglais, par Mme. La Baronne Isabelle de Montolieu. Orné de figures. Paris . . . 1828. 3 vols. 12°.

1816. La Nouvelle Emma, ou les Caractères Anglais du Siècle, par l'auteur d'Orgueil et Préjugé, &c., &c. Traduit de l'anglais. Paris . . . 1816. 4 vols. 12°.

1816. Le Parc de Mansfield, ou Les Trois Cousines, par l'auteur de Raison et Sensibilité, ou Les Deux Manières d'Aimer, d'Orgueil et Préjugé, &c. Traduit de l'anglais, par M. Henri V******n [Villemain]. Paris . . . 1816. 4 vols. 12°.

1821. La Famille Elliot, ou l'Ancienne Inclination, traduction libre de l'anglais d'un roman posthume de Miss Jane Austen, auteur de Raison et Sensibilité, d'Orgueil et Préjugé, d'Emma, de Mansfield-Parc, &c. Par Mme de Montolieu. Avec figures. Paris . . . 1821. 2 vols. 8°.

This is the first appearance of J. A.'s name on a title-page. It includes 'Notice biographique sur Jane Austen traduite de l'anglais'. The translator explains that the title *Persuasion* 'm'a paru trop vague en français; je ne trouvais pas qu'il indiquât l'ensemble de la situation'.

1828. La Famille Elliot [&c., much as in 1821]. Nouvelle édition, ornée de figures. Paris . . . 1828. 2 vols. 8°.

1822. Orgueil et Prévention, Par l'Auteur de Raison et Sensibilité; traduit de l'anglais Par Mlle É . . .*** [Éloïse Perks]. Paris . . . 1822. 3 vols. 12°.

1822. Orgueil et Préjugé. Par l'Auteur de Raison et Sensibilité. Traduit de l'anglois. Paris . . . 1822. 4 vols. 8°.

1824. L'Abbaye de Northanger; Traduit de l'anglais de Jeanne Austen, auteur d'Orgueil et Préjugé, du Parc de Mansfield, de la Famille Elliot, de la Nouvelle Emma, etc. Par Mme. Hyacinthe de F**** [Ferrières]. Paris . . . 1824. 3 vols. 12°.

1882. Miss Austen. Persuasion. Roman traduit de l'anglais par Mme Letorsay. Paris. 1882.

1899. Jane Austen. Catherine Morland, roman traduit de l'anglais par Félix Fénéon. Paris 1899.

1910. Emma. Traduit de l'anglais par Pierre de Puliga. Paris 1910.

1933. Emma traduit par P. et E. de Saint-Segond. Paris. 1933.

After 1945, as after 1815, French and Belgian interest in the novels was shown by translations of all of them: not all new, but all independent of the earliest versions. *Raison et Sensibilité* (Brussels 1945); *Marianne et Elinor* (Paris 1948); *Orgueil et Préjugés*, or *Prévention* (Brussels 1945, Paris 1946, 1947); *Mansfield Park* (Brussels 1945); *Emma* (Brussels 1945); *Catherine Morland* (Paris 1945, a reprint of 1933); *Persuasion* (Paris 1945).

20. SPANISH

1919. Persuasion. Translated by Ortega y Gasset. Madrid 1899.

1921. La Abadía de Northanger. Translated by I. Oyarzabal. Madrid. 1921.

1924. Orgullo y Perjuicio. Translated by J. J. de Urrias. Madrid 1924.

20a. ITALIAN

1935. Orgoglio e pregiudizio. Torino.

21. GERMAN

1939. Elisabeth und Darcy, translated by Karin von Schab. 1939.

1948. Stolz und Vorurteil, Die Abtei von Northanger, Anne Elliot, translated by M. Rauchenberger. Köln. 1948.

22. FINNISH

Pride and Prejudice, Emma, Persuasion. Helsinki 1949–51.

II

MINOR WORKS

(1) JUVENILIA

A COLLECTED edition in J. A.'s hand has been preserved. It is in
three uniform volumes entitled 'Volume the First' (Bodleian),
Volume the Second (a descendant of Sir Francis Austen), Volume
the Third (R. A. Austen-Leigh). Many of the pieces are dated
or datable 1790–3 (J. A. was born 1775). But since the pieces
are not in chronological order it follows that our MS. is not the
original but a later collection. This we cannot date; but there is a
correction as late as 1811—the mention in Volume the Third of
Hannah More's *Coelebs*, 1811.

23. 1922. Love and Freindship and Other Early Works . . . by
Jane Austen. With a Preface by G. K. Chesterton. Chatto &
Windus, 1922. 8°. 260 copies were printed on hand-made large
paper.

Keynes 173. This is Volume the Second. The coloured portraits of
Kings and Queens, by Cassandra Austen, which in the MS. are prefixed to
each chapter of 'The History of England' (from Henry IV to Charles I)
are here assembled as endpapers. The MS. is owned by a descendant of
Sir Francis Austen.

24. 1932. Volume the First by Jane Austen. Now first printed
. . . Oxford 1932. Edited by R. W. C. 8°. An edition of 100
copies in a distinctive binding has two facsimiles.

25. 1951. Volume the Third by Jane Austen. Now first
printed . . . Oxford 1951. Edited by R. W. C. 8°.

This volume includes a contribution to 'Evelyn' by J. A. E. L.
(which I misprinted J. E. A. L., confounding sister with brother), i.e.
J. A.'s niece Jane Anna Elizabeth Lefroy, James Austen's elder daughter.

II (2)

THE WATSONS, LADY SUSAN, THE CANCELLED ENDING OF PERSUASION, SANDITON

THE WATSONS

26. 1803 or later (the MS. has a watermark of 1803). The fragment traditionally known as *The Watsons* (the MS. has no title) was first published in the *Memoir* 1871. One quire of the MS. was given to a Red Cross sale in 1918 by the late William Austen-Leigh, and is now in the Pierpont Morgan Library. The remainder belongs to W. A.-L.'s legatees.

Memoir 1871, 364 (or 1926, 121): 'When the author's sister, Cassandra, showed the manuscript of the work to some of her nieces, she also told them something of the intended story. . . . Mr. Watson was soon to die; and Emma to become dependent for a home on her narrow-minded sister-in-law and brother. She was to decline an offer of marriage from Lord Osborne, and much of the interest of the tale was to arise from Lady [? Miss] Osborne's love for Mr. Howard, and his counter affection for Emma, whom he was finally to marry.'

The late John Hubback, a grandson of Sir Francis Austen, wrote to *The Times Lit. Suppt.* 24 May 1928 that J. E. Austen-Leigh 'was supplied with this information . . . by my mother. . . . Although she had no access to the manuscript . . . after her marriage in 1842, she based "The Younger Sister" (1850) on her memories of that manuscript and of all that Cassandra (who died in 1845) had told her nieces at Portsdown. Every item in the paragraph . . . is worked out in "The Younger Sister", and supplemented from her own fertile imagination, in part.' See 27.

1927. The Watsons a Fragment by Jane Austen Now Reprinted from the Manuscript. Oxford 1927. 8°. An edition of

250 copies on hand-made paper includes a facsimile of one page of the MS.

27. 1928. Edith and Francis Brown. The Watsons by Jane Austen. Completed in accordance with her intentions, by Edith (her great grand-niece) and Francis Brown. 1928.

I include this because I believe it is the only 'continuation' that claims to be based on knowledge of J. A.'s intentions. Mrs. Brown's story (for the foundation of which see 26) is as follows. Her grandmother Mrs. Hubback was Catherine, daughter of Francis Austen. She was born too late to know J. A., but lived much with her aunt Cassandra, on whose information she built the three volumes of *The Younger Sister*. 'The first was Jane Austen through a haze of memory. Jane Austen incidents in the second. No connexion with Jane Austen in the third. . . . We have tried to disentangle Jane's story from that of her niece.'

Readers will form their own judgement of the disentanglement. Mrs. Brown makes one conjecture that deserves record. The story of the Watsons opens with a date: 'Tuesday Octr ye 13th'. Mrs. Brown's guess is that this is the date on which J. A. took up her pen; 13 Oct. was a Tuesday in 1807. The author of the *Memoir* (1871, 67) stated that the story 'must have been written' at Bath—that is before 1806. But later (p. 295) he was content to think it 'probable' that a MS. with a watermark of 1803 was written within a year or two.

LADY SUSAN

28. *c.* 1805. The piece traditionally known as *Lady Susan* (the MS. has no title) was first published in the *Memoir* 1871, from a copy, and reprinted in Bentley's collection from 1879.

1925. Lady Susan by Jane Austen. . . . Reprinted from the Manuscript [then in the possession of the fifth Earl of Rosebery]. Oxford 1925. 8°. An edition of 250 copies was printed on hand-made paper.

CANCELLED ENDING OF *PERSUASION*

29. 1816. The only surviving MS. of the six novels consists of the first draft of the conclusion of *Persuasion*: chapters 10 and 11 of the second volume (volume IV of *N.A. and P.*). The dates on the MS. (British Museum) are 8, 16, and 18 July 1816. The MS. was first published in the *Memoir* 1871, where the author stated (p. 157) that J. A. 'cancelled the condemned chapter, and wrote two others, entirely different, in its stead'. This is inaccurate; more than a quarter of 'chapter 10' is substantially, and for the most part verbally, identical with the print of 1818. The final chapter was retained, with some changes, to become chapter 12.

1926. Two Chapters of Persuasion printed from Jane Austen's Autograph. Oxford 1926. 8°. An edition of 250 copies on handmade paper includes a facsimile of the entire MS. The editor (R. W. C.) records in his notes all verbal variations between the MS. of 'chapter 11' and the 1818 text of chapter 12.

SANDITON

30. 1817. The fragment traditionally known as *Sanditon* (the MS. has no title) was described, as The Last Work, in the *Memoir* 1871 (see 82), with extracts. The MS. was given to J. A.'s niece Anna Lefroy, whose descendant, the late Isabel Lefroy, allowed me to publish it. She later gave it to King's College, Cambridge, of which her kinsman Augustus Austen-Leigh had been Provost. See 132 (Forster).

1925. Fragment of a Novel written by Jane Austen January— March 1817. Now first printed from the Manuscript. Oxford 1925. 8°. An edition of 250 copies on hand-made paper includes a facsimile of a page of the MS.

II (3)

MISCELLANEOUS

CHARADES

31. n.d. Charades written a hundred years ago by Jane Austen and her Family. Spottiswoode & Co., n.d., but preface dated June 1895. Two issues, one priced 1*s*. 6*d*., the other presumably for private circulation. Reprinted in *Personal Aspects* 1920 (126).

'A hundred years ago' must be called a guess, for one piece is by James Edward, born 1798. Of the 22 charades three, Nos. 18–20, are by J. A. I have not traced the MS.; but Mr. R. A. Austen-Leigh owns a MS. (with a dated watermark 18–7; the third digit has never escaped the abhorrèd shears—I guess 1807) containing these 22 charades and 22 others. Though the texts are not quite identical, it is possible that 1895 is a selection and that the printer worked from a copy, which might not survive.

Another MS., formerly in the collection described in *Times Lit. Suppt.* 14 Jan. 1926 and now in my possession, is inscribed 'Cass Eliz^th Austen' and is probably (in whole or in part) in her hand. The watermark is 1798. This contains 19 pieces (either 'Charade' or 'Riddle'), none assigned to an author. Three of these are in 1895, and one is in the Austen-Leigh MS. but not in 1895.

OTHER VERSES

32. So far as is known, J. A.'s only attempt at serious versification was the lines on the death of Anne Lefroy, her very dear friend, who was accidentally killed in 1804. These are quoted in chapter III of the *Memoir* (81). A number of other verses have survived; these are all more or less comic, and often extemporized. I hope to include them all in a forthcoming collection of the Minor Works. For J. A.'s Charades see 31. There are occasional verses in the Juvenilia.

Minor Works

33. *c.* 1816. Plan of a Novel according to Hints from Various Quarters by Jane Austen with Opinions on Mansfield Park and Emma collected and transcribed by her and other Documents. Oxford 1926.

Keynes 179. *Facts and Problems* 164. These documents came from the collection described in *Times Lit. Suppt.* 14 Jan. 1926. The *Plan* and the letters that occasioned it are in the British Museum, the *Opinions* in the Pierpont Morgan Library. The *Plan* had been printed imperfectly in *Memoir* 1871, fully in *Life*. The *Opinions* of *Emma* are in the *Life*, those in *M.P.* had been quoted only.

PRAYERS

The collection described in *Times Lit. Suppt.* 14 Jan. 1926 included three prayers in two MSS. The first MS. is inscribed 'Prayers composed by my ever dear sister Jane' and is water-marked 1818; J. A. died in 1817. The hand is almost certainly Cassandra's. The second MS. has no clue to its date; it is partly in a hand which may be Henry Austen's, partly in a hand that has been thought by experts to be Jane's own.

34. 1940. The Prayers were published by Mr. William Matson Roth at the Colt Press of San Francisco, with a facsimile of a page thought to be partly in J. A.'s hand.

Addendum

34a. Works. Volume VI (see 18). Minor Works now first collected and edited by R. W. Chapman. 1954.

III

LETTERS

UNTIL the publication in 1932 of the first edition (below) aiming at completeness, J. A.'s letters had been published in three books: the *Memoir* of 1870 (81), Lord Brabourne's collection of 1884 (95), and *Jane Austen's Sailor Brothers* 1906 (114). Almost all the letters then available were quoted, in whole or in part, by W. and R. A. Austen-Leigh in the *Life* 1913 (120).

35. 1932. Jane Austen's Letters to her sister Cassandra and others collected and edited by R. W. Chapman. Oxford 1932.

This edition was based in the main on the autographs, but for many letters depended on the texts of 1884. It includes an essay on J. A. as a letter-writer, notes, and very full indexes. The index of authors and books is inferior, as a survey of J. A.'s reading, to the index of Literary Allusions in volume V of my edition of the novels, which comprehends, in its current issue, the minor works and the letters as well as the six novels. The illustrations, as in my edition of the novels, are all from contemporary documents. They include a facsimile of a letter, portraits, views of various Austen houses, and maps of Hampshire and Kent. The frontispiece is from a drawing of a seated lady, signed and dated 1804 (not 1794 as I unhappily printed in 1932) by Cassandra Austen. My confident conjecture that the subject was her sister has since been confirmed (*Facts and Problems* 213).

I printed a few copies of the important letter to Martha Lloyd of 16 Feb. 1813 (see above, 6), which became available in 1933. It is included in my second edition below.

The edition is in two volumes, or one on India paper.

36. 1952. Jane Austen's Letters [&c. as 1932].

This edition in one volume incorporates a few corrections and adds No. 78.1 (see above). A last-minute addition (and therefore not indexed) was the very interesting letter (99.1) to Martha Lloyd of 2 Sept. 1814, which includes some reflection on politics, religion, and 'the Americans'.

37. 1924. Five Letters from Jane Austen to her Niece Fanny Knight printed in facsimile. Oxford 1924. See 95.

IV

AUTOBIOGRAPHY

APART from her letters and the 1816 Advertisement to *N.A.* (9), only a few scraps remain that can be called autobiographical.

38. 1816. Note of the dates of composition of *M.P.*, *P.*, and *E.* (in that order, though the dates for *E.* are earlier than those for *P.*). Facsimile in *Plan of a Novel* 1926 (33).

1817. 'Profits of my Novels, over and above the £600 in the Navy Fives'. The total to March 1817 is £84. 13s. 0d. Facsimile (as above). Both scraps are in the Pierpont Morgan Library.

[n.d. Memorandum by Cassandra Austen, quoted *Life* 96. Dates of composition of *First Impressions*, *S. and S.*, *N.A.*

Life 96; *Facts and Problems* 42. Mrs. Henry Burke. The words 'probably called Susan', which in the *Life* follow 'Northanger Abbey', are editorial.]

V

BIOGRAPHY AND CRITICISM

39. *c.* 1785–1803. SIR SAMUEL EGERTON BRYDGES. *Autobiography* 1834, ii. 40–41.

'I remember Jane Austen, the novelist, a little child: she was very intimate with Mrs. Lefroy (his sister). . . . When I knew Jane Austen I never suspected that she was an authoress; but my eyes told me that she was fair and handsome, slight and elegant, but with cheeks a little too full. The last time I think that I saw her was at Ramsgate in 1803.'

J. A. in a letter refers to S. E. B. as 'Egerton'.

40. *c.* 1811. ? JAMES EDWARD AUSTEN. Unpublished. 'To Miss Jane Austen the reputed Author of "Sense and Sensibility", a Novel lately publish'd.'

> 'On such Subjects no Wonder that she shou'd write well,
> In whom so united those Qualities dwell;
> Where "dear Sensibility", Sterne's darling Maid,
> With Sense so attemper'd is finely pourtray'd.
> Fair Elinor's Self in that Mind is exprest,
> And the Feelings of Marianne live in that Breast.
> Oh then, gentle Lady! continue to write,
> And the Sense of your Readers t'amuse & delight.
>
> A Friend.'

This letter is addressed to Miss Jane Austen and bears the Alton postmark. It came from the collection described in *Times Lit. Suppt.* 14 Jan. 1926 (20*a*) and is now in my possession. My guess is that the author was James Edward Austen, who was born in 1798. The lines were presumably written before the publication of *P. and P.* in 1813. The writing might well be that of a precocious boy of about thirteen. A much longer poetical tribute by him, 'not quite yet fifteen years old', is printed in Mary Augusta Austen-Leigh's *Personal Aspects of Jane Austen* 1920, 149 (126); this is known to be James Edward's. See also 43, 78, 81–83, 119.

41. 1813. RICHARD BRINSLEY SHERIDAN. MS. in British Museum (formerly in the collection described in *Times Lit. Suppt.* 14 Jan. 1926): part of a letter to Cassandra Austen.

'Miss Shirreff told me she was dining at . . . Mr. Whitbreads when Pride & P. came out; she was sitting next to Mr. Sheridan, who asked her if she had seen it, and advised her to buy it immediately, for it was one of the cleverest things he ever read.'

42. c. 1814. ROBERT SOUTHEY. Reported by Henry Austen's friend Henry Sandford (see Index to *Letters* 1932). MS. in British Museum (formerly in the collection described in *T.L.S.* 14 Jan. 1926). This is part of a letter (n.d.) from H. A. to Cassandra; my date depends on the assumption that he would have written to J. A. herself if she had been alive. But see p. 57.

'I will relate to you in his own words what he said to me yesterday. "Some few years ago I paid a visit to Mr. Herries at Montreal. Mr. Southey was among the visitors also. When I orderd my chaise for London, I asked if any person wished for a cast. Southey accepted the offer. At the foot of Maranscourt[1] hill something induced me to make a remark which was in fact a quotation from one of your Sister's Novels. Southey immediately exclaimed 'that's in Miss Austen's Novels.' 'What said I to Southey, 'Do you know Miss Austen's works?' 'Do I know them replied S—. Sir, It would take me to the top of that hill before I could tell you whether I had rather be the Author of Miss Austen's novels, or Walter Scott's.' " '

43. c. 1815. ? JAMES EDWARD AUSTEN. Unpublished.

'An admirer of Miss Austin's Novels, entreats her, in the next edition of Mansfield Park to add another volume, in which the example of useful, and amiable maried [*sic*] life may be exhibited in the characters of Edmund & Fanny.—The Novel has but one fault;—it is too

---

[1] So it may be read. The hill, as its neighbour Lord Stanhope tells me, has been variously named. Once Maggoty Bank, it was promoted (by 'Citizen' Stanhope, who made a road) to Madam's Court or Morant's Court, and is now usually Star Hill. As it climbs from 300 feet to 695, Southey had plenty of time. See also 51, 55.

quickly read; and one laments that his acquaintance with persons so amiable and elegant in mind and manners is of so short duration.—'

This unsigned letter is addressed Miss Austin Alton Hants and bears the Alton penny postmark. It came from the same collection as the preceding tribute, and is in my possession. See also 40, 78, 81–83, 119.

44. 1815. (Presumably) HENRY STEPHEN FOX, nephew of Charles James Fox. MS. in British Museum (formerly in the collection described in *Times Lit. Suppt.* 14 Jan. 1926): endorsed by a child of Charles James Austen 'Extract from a letter dated Palermo, May 6th, 1815, from my Father to Aunt Jane'.

'Books became the subject of conversation. I praised Waverly highly; when a young man present, observed that nothing had come out for years, to be compared with Pride & Prejudice, Sense & Sensibility &c. As I am sure you must be anxious to know the name of a person of so much taste, I should tell you it is Fox, a nephew of the late Charles James Fox.'

45. 1815+. Accounts quoted by MARY RUSSELL MITFORD in her *Life* by A. G. L'Estrange 1870, i. 305, 331; ii. 13, 39.

(To Sir William Elford, April 3, 1815.—)

'I have discovered that our great favourite Miss Austen is my countrywoman; that Mama knew all her family very intimately; and that she herself is an old maid (I beg her pardon—I mean a young lady) with whom Mama before her marriage was acquainted. Mama says she was then the prettiest, silliest, most affected husband-hunting butterfly she ever remembers and a friend of mine who visits her now says that she has stiffened into the most perpendicular, precise, taciturn piece of "single blessedness" that ever existed, and that till "Pride and Prejudice" showed what a precious gem was hidden in that unbending case, she was no more regarded in society than a poker or a fire screen or any other thin, upright piece of wood or iron that fills its corner in peace and quiet. The case is very different now; she is still a poker but a poker of whom everyone is afraid. It must be confessed that this silent observation from such an observer is rather formidable . . . a wit, a delineator of character who does not talk is formidable indeed.'

In later letters Miss Mitford relents. In 1816 'how delightful is her Emma!'; in 1817 the death of 'our Miss Austen' is 'a terrible loss'; in 1818 she is 'our dear Miss Austen'. See also 68.

The author of the *Memoir* in a postscript to the first edition (not in the second, but see the 1926 edition 209) confuted the story of M. R. M.'s mother on the ground that when her father, Dr. Russell, Rector of Ashe near Steventon, died in 1783, his widow and daughter left the neighbourhood, and 'all intercourse between the families ceased'. J. A. was then not eight years old. For the poisoned source of the account of J. A. in later life see *Facts and Problems* 120, or *Letters* s.v. Baverstock. The author of the *Memoir* did not discuss this, since 'Miss Mitford candidly expresses a doubt whether she had not been misinformed'.

46. 1816, before March. WALTER SCOTT. Review of *Emma* in *Quarterly Review* xiv, '1815', but not issued until March 1816 (Keynes 256). See also 49, 50, 53. The review deals at length in generalities about novels, and gives the plots of *S. and S.*, *P. and P.* (not, as J. A. regretted, of *M.P.*), and of *E.*, with long quotations from the last.

'The author of *Emma* . . . has produced sketches of such spirit and originality, that we never miss the excitation which depends upon a narrative of uncommon events.'

'The author's knowledge of the world, and the peculiar tact with which she presents characters that the reader cannot fail to recognize, reminds us something of the merits of the Flemish school of painting.'

'. . . the merits and faults of the author. The former consists [*sic*] in the force of a narrative conducted with much neatness and point, and a quiet yet comic dialogue, in which the characters of the speakers evolve themselves with dramatic effect. The faults . . . arise from the minute detail which the author's plan comprehends.' Scott goes on to complain

22

that 'characters of folly and simplicity, such as those of old Woodhouse and Miss Bates', are 'apt to become as tiresome in fiction as in real society'. This stricture has not been endorsed by posterity. It rebounds against such characters as Lady Margaret in *Old Mortality*, with her repetition of 'his sacred majesty's disjeune'.

47. 1818, 1833. HENRY THOMAS AUSTEN. The 'Biographical Notice of the Author', prefixed to the posthumous edition of *N.A. and P.*, is anonymous. It is of some 2,500 words. In Bentley's edition of 1833, where it is dated October 1832 and is expanded to some 3,100, a note (quoted Keynes 27) ascribes it to 'the author's brother, the Rev. Mr. Austen'; this can only mean Henry Thomas Austen, since the other parson brother, James, had died in 1819.

Facts and Problems 168.

48. 1821. RICHARD WHATELY. Review of a 'new edition' of *N.A. and P.* in *Quarterly Review* 1821 (vol. xxiv, 'October and January'), 352. Reprinted 1862 in his *Miscellaneous Reviews*, which ascertain the authorship.

'Miss Austin [*sic*] has the merit (in our judgment most essential) of being evidently a Christian writer: a merit which is much enhanced . . . by her religion being not at all obtrusive.'

Her dialogue 'she conducts with a regard to character hardly exceeded even by Shakspeare himself'.

49. 1822. SIR WALTER SCOTT. Letter 10 Feb. 1822 to Joanna Baillie. Lockhart 1837, v. 158.

'Did you know Miss Austen, authoress of some novels which have a good deal of nature in them?—nature in ordinary and middle life, to be sure, but valuable from its strong resemblance and correct drawing.' See also 46, 50, 53.

50. 1826. SIR WALTER SCOTT. *Journal* 14 and 28 Mar. Lockhart 1837, vi. 264, 281. *Journal* ed. J. G. Tait 1939, i. 135.

14 Mar. 'Read again, and for the third time at least, Miss Austen's very finely written novel of Pride and Prejudice. That young lady had a talent for describing the involvements, and feelings, and characters of ordinary life, which is to me the most wonderful I ever met with. The Big Bow-wow strain I can do myself like any now going; but the exquisite touch, which renders ordinary commonplace things and characters interesting, from the truth of the description and the sentiment, is denied to me. What a pity such a gifted creature died so early!'

28 Mar. 'The women do this better; Edgeworth, Ferrier, Austen, have all given portraits of real society, far superior to any thing man, vain man, has produced of the like nature.'

Cassandra Austen made a copy of the first of these passages: *Times Lit. Suppt.* 14 Jan. 1926, 19a, MS. in British Museum. See also 46, 49, 53.

51. 1830. ROBERT SOUTHEY in Brydges, *Autobiography* (see 39) ii. 269: Letter of 8 Apr. 1830.

'You mention Miss Austen; her novels are more true to nature, and have (for my sympathies) passages of finer feeling than any others of this age.' See also 42, 55.

52. 1830. SIR JAMES MACKINTOSH and MADAME DE STAËL. *Memoirs* of M. by his son Robert James 1835, ii. 471.

'There was genius in the sketching out that new kind of novel. . . . It was impossible for a foreigner to understand fully the merit of her works. Madame de Staël to whom he had recommended one of her novels, found no interest in it, and in her note to him in reply said it was "vulgaire", and yet he said nothing could be more true than what he wrote in answer,—*"there is no book which that word would suit so little"*.'

53. 1831. SIR WALTER SCOTT. Quoted by Mrs. John Davy, in Lockhart 1837, vii. 338.

'There's a finishing-off in some of her scenes that is really quite above every body else.' See also 46, 49, 50.

54. 1834. ANTHONY TROLLOPE in his *Autobiography* 1883, i. 55.

'I had already [at nineteen] made up my mind that *Pride and Prejudice* was the best novel in the English language' (later he preferred *Esmond*).

55. 1834. *Memoirs and Letters of Sara Coleridge* edited by her Daughter 1873, i. 75.

Letter of Aug. —, 1834 to Emily Trevenen

'Jane Austen . . . if not the greatest is surely the most faultless of female novelists. My uncle Southey and my father had an equally high opinion of her merits, but Mr. Wordsworth used to say that though he admitted that her novels were an admirable copy of life, he could not be interested in productions of that kind; unless the truth of nature were presented to him clarified, as it were, by the pervading light of imagination, it had scarce any attractions in his eyes.' See also 42, 51.

56. 1835. GEORGE WILLIAM FREDERICK HOWARD, styled Viscount Morpeth (later seventh Earl of Carlisle). 'The Lady and the Novel' in *The Keepsake for MDCCCXXXV* (not 1825 as in *Memoir*) 27.

He apostrophizes 'thou, all perfect Austen.' . . .
> 'While the clear style flows on without pretence,
> With unstained purity, and unmatched sense.'

57. 1837. JOHN HENRY NEWMAN. *Letters . . . of John Henry Newman* edited Anne Mozley 1891, ii. 223.

'I have been reading "Emma". Everything Miss Austen writes is clever, but I desiderate something. There is a want of *body* to the story. . . . There are some beautiful things in it. Emma herself is the most interesting to me of all her heroines. I feel kind to her whenever I think of her. But Miss Austen has no romance—none at all. What vile creatures her parsons are! she has not a dream of the high Catholic $\mathring{\eta}\theta o\varsigma$. That other woman, Fairfax, is a dolt—but I like Emma.'

58. 1840. JAMES BOWLING MOZLEY. Letter 5 May 1840 to Anne Mozley. *Letters of J.B.M.* 1885, 106.

'H. E. M. has found that Mr. Fowle, whom you know, is cousin of our favourite, Miss Austin [*sic*]. Harriet, of course, asked a great many questions, and made out that she was an exceedingly nice, amiable, pretty person, just what one would wish her to be.'

Harriet Elizabeth, Mrs. Thomas Mozley, was J. H. Newman's sister. For the Austen–Fowle connexion see *Letters*.

58a. 1841. HENRY WILLIAM WILBERFORCE in *The British Critic* lix, 1841, 187.

'It cannot be denied that Miss Austen's heroines are in general underbred. Emma is a vulgar rich girl, who would be absolutely intolerable when she lost the advantages of youth and beauty; the Miss Bennetts are coarse in high degree, admirably as they are drawn.'

59. 1842. PHILARÈTE CHASLES, 'Du Roman en Angleterre depuis Walter Scott', *Rev. des deux Mondes* 15 July 1842.

'Miss Austen déploya un mélange de sensibilité douce. . . . Entre ces romancières [Burney, Ferrier, J. A.], il n y à guère que des nuances et des demi-teintes. L'imagination n'est par leur fort. La malice féminine, la pruderie puritaine, la tradition de la moralité prêchée par Richardson, et l'étude un peu maladive du cœur humain et des caractères, regnent dans ces œuvres délicates et gracieuses . . . ce sont les petite-filles de Richardson.

Ce n'est pas que, fidèle à la tradition de sa race et de son milieu, Jane Austen ne jouisse profondément de la beauté d'un site, de la grâce d'un paysage. Ce qu'elle blâme dans le culte et la recherche du pittoresque, c'est qu'il s'attache à l'exceptionnel. . . .' (331).

60. 1843. JANE WELSH CARLYLE: a letter of March 1843 in *Letters and Memorials* 1883, i. 186.

' "Miss Austin?" "Too washy; water-gruel for mind and body at the same time were too bad".'

61. 1843. ANNE KATHARINE ELWOOD. *Memoirs of the Literary Ladies of England* 1843, ii. 174–86, Jane Austen.

This though of little intrinsic interest—it consists largely of quotations from the prefatory matter of 1818 (9)— deserves mention as the earliest estimate of any length or from outside the family. Mrs. Elwood was well informed; she quotes Scott (50) and the *Edinburgh Review* (62).

62. 1843. THOMAS BABINGTON MACAULAY. *Edinburgh Review* lxxvi, Jan. 1843, 561, in article on Mme D'Arblay (anon., but later acknowledged).

Shakespeare 'has scarcely left us a single caricature. Shakspeare has had neither equal nor second. But among the writers who, in the point which we have mentioned, have approached nearest to the manner of the great master, we have no hesitation in placing Jane Austen'. Macaulay goes on to note the nice, and unexpected, discrimination of four parsons: Ferrars, Tilney, Bertram, Elton. 'Harpagon is not more unlike Jourdain . . . than every one of Miss Austen's young divines to all their reverend brethren. And almost all this is done by touches so delicate, that they elude analysis.' See also 70.

63. 1847. GEORGE HENRY LEWES. 'Recent Novels' (including *Jane Eyre*) in *Fraser's Magazine* xxxvi, Dec. 1847, 687.

Shakespeare and Scott. 'The two minds had certainly some peculiarities in common, but they belonged altogether to a different species. Now Miss Austen has been called a prose Shakspeare; and, among others, by Macaulay. In spite of the sense of incongruity which besets us in the words *prose* Shakspeare, we confess the greatness of Miss Austen, her marvellous dramatic power, seems more than any thing in Scott akin to the highest quality in Shakspeare.' See also 65, 67, 72.

64. 1848. CHARLOTTE BRONTË in Elizabeth Cleghorn Gaskell *Life of Charlotte Brontë* 1857. Letter 11 Jan. 1848 to G. H. Lewes.

'Why do you like Miss Austen so very much? I am puzzled on that point. . . . I had not seen 'Pride and Prejudice' till I read that sentence of yours, and then I got the book. And what did I find? An accurate daguerrotyped portrait of a commonplace face; a carefully-fenced, highly-cultivated garden, with neat borders and delicate flowers; but no glance of a bright vivid physiognomy, no open country, no fresh air; no blue hill, no bonny beck. I should hardly like to live with her ladies and gentlemen, in their elegant but confined houses'. (She can) 'understand admiration of George Sand . . . she is sagacious and profound—Miss Austen is only shrewd and observant.'

More to the same purpose, 18 Jan. Lewes had explained that J. A. lacks poetry and 'sentiment' (his marks of quotation). C. B. replies that without these no writer can be great; it is poetry that 'elevates' George Sand, sentiment that 'extracts the venom' from Thackeray.

65. *c.* 1850. GEORGE HENRY LEWES in *Leader* (1850–1860), quoted in Anna T. Kitchel, *George Lewes and George Eliot*, New York 1933, 104.

Shakespeare in 'the power of constructing and animating character may truly be said to find a younger sister in Miss Austen. Observe, however, that in place of his poetry we must put her daring prose—daring from its humble truthfulness.' See also 63, 67, 72.

66. ? *c.* 1850. THOMAS CARLYLE quoted by Francis Espinasse, *Literary Recollections* 1893, 216.

'Anthony Trollope's novels he compared to "alum", and Jane Austen's, so bepraised by Macaulay, he summarily dismissed as mere "dish-washings!"'

My date is a guess. David Alec Wilson quotes the passage in *Carlyle at his Zenith 1848–53*, 1927. The judgement on Trollope must of course be later.

67. 1852. GEORGE HENRY LEWES, 'The Lady Novelists', *Westminster Review* July 1852, 134.

'. . . the greatest artist that has ever written, using the term to signify the most perfect mastery over the means to her end . . . out of Shakespeare it would be difficult to find characters so typical yet so nicely demarcated within the limits of their kind.'

This article is included without comment in *Essays and Reviews of George Eliot*, Boston 1887. But Gordon S. Haight, *George Eliot and John Chapman*, Yale Univ. Press 1940, 44, 57, seems decisive in favour of Lewes. See also 63, 65, 72.

68. 1852. MARY RUSSELL MITFORD. *Recollections of a Literary Life* 1852, ii. 197.

'Her exquisite story of "Persuasion" absolutely haunted me. . . . I doubt if anyone, even Scott himself, have left such perfect impressions of character and place.' See also 45.

69. 1853. *North American Review* lxxvii, July 1853, 201. 'Thackeray as a Novelist', Anon., but attributed in the Index, 1878, to J[ohn] F[oster] Kirk.

J. A. not well known in America. 'We have never read the work (*S. and S.*) without astonishment that the most subtle play of motives, and the most delicate traits of character should have been thus faithfully portrayed by a woman at the age of twenty-five.'

69a. 1853. *Christian Remembrancer* xxvi. 33.

' "A writer of the school of Miss Austen" is a much-abused phrase, applied now-a-days by critics who, it is charitable to suppose, have never read Miss Austen's works, to any female writer who composes dull stories without incidents, full of level conversation, and concerned with characters of middle life.'

70. 1858. THOMAS BABINGTON MACAULAY. In Sir George Trevelyan's *Life* 1875, ii. 466.

'He never for a moment wavered in his allegiance to Miss Austen. In 1858 he notes in his journal: "If I could get materials I really would write a short life of that wonderful woman".' See also 62.

71. 1858. LOUISA DOROTHEA STANLEY, writing to a niece, in *The Amberley Papers* edited by Bertrand and Patricia Russell 1937, i. 54.

'I think "*Revolting*" not at all the term to use in speaking of the personages in Miss Austin's Novels—poor Mrs. Jennings is not high bred— & Miss Lucy is very odious—but *Revolting* is a strong word & wd. better suit some of the painfully bad characters in Thackeray or Dickens.'

72. 1859. Blackwood's *Edinburgh Magazine* lxxxvi, 1859, 99. The writer, as Messrs. Blackwood courteously inform me, was G. H. Lewes.

'Beyond the literary circle we find the name almost entirely unknown' and apt to be confused with a translating Mrs. Austin. . . . 'Her place is among the Immortals; but the pedestal is erected in a quiet niche of the great temple.' See also 63, 65, 67.

73. 1860. W. F. P. [SIR WILLIAM FREDERICK POLLOCK]. 'British Novelists—Richardson, Miss Austen, Scott' in *Fraser's Magazine* lxi, 1860, 30.

A sustained eulogy. J. A. is, 'of all his successors', the nearest Richardson, 'in the power of impressing reality'. She 'has been accused of writing dull stories about ordinary people. But her supposed ordinary people are really not such very ordinary people'. 'No instance occurs of a scene in which men only are present' (I thought that was *my* discovery). 'The machinery of representation is almost wholly concealed'. *S. and S.* 'has perhaps more of movement than its successors, and in no other is there a

character of so much passionate tenderness as belongs to Marianne'. *E.*
'will generally be recognized . . . as the best of her works. In delicate
investigation of the nicer peculiarities of character, and in its perfectly
finished execution, it cannot be surpassed'.

74. 1860. EDWARD FITZGERALD, Letter to W. F. Pollock
23 Feb. 1860. *Works* 1903, ii. 111.

'I laid out half a crown on your Fraser (see 73): and liked much of it
very much: especially the Beginning about the Advantage the Novelist
has over the Play-writer. A little too much always about Miss Austen,
whom yet I think quite capital in a Circle I have found quite unendur-
able to walk in. . . . I have been very glad to find I could take to a Novel
again, in Trollope's Barchester Towers, etc.: not perfect, like Miss
Austen: but then so much wider Scope: and perfect enough to make me
feel I know the People though caricatured or carelessly drawn.'

75. ? 1860. ALFRED TENNYSON. *Autobiography of Henry Taylor*
1885, ii. 193. Mrs. Cameron in an undated letter.

'Alfred talked very pleasantly that evening to Annie Thackeray and
L— S —. He spoke of Jane Austen, as James Spedding does, as next to
Shakespeare ! . . . he thanked God Almighty with his whole heart that
he knew nothing, and that the world knew nothing of Jane Austen,
and that there were no letters preserved either of Shakespeare's or of
Jane Austen's, that they had not been ripped open like pigs.' See also
79, 105.

76. 1862. JULIA KAVANAGH. *English Women of Letters* ii. 235
(in edition 1863).

'What her extraordinary powers wanted in extent, they made up in
depth.'

77. 1863. MRS. R[OBERT] C[ASSIE] WATERSTON (Anna Cabot
Lowell Quincey) in *Atlantic Monthly* xi, 1863, 235.

An enthusiastic article, quoting Scott, Macaulay, and others.

78. 1865 [JAMES EDWARD AUSTEN-LEIGH]. *Recollections of the Early Days of the Vine Hunt . . .* by a Sexagenarian 1865.

This scarce little book has some entertaining particulars of people who belonged to the Austen circle in Hampshire. See also 40, 43, 81–83, 119.

79. August 1867. ALFRED TENNYSON.

    1. SIR CHARLES BRUCE LOCKER TENNYSON. *Alfred Tennyson* 1949, 373.

Tennyson at Lyme, to Palgrave: 'Now take me to the Cobb, and show me the steps where Louisa Musgrove fell.'

    2. FRANCIS TURNER PALGRAVE. Jane Austen and Lyme, in *The Grove, a Monthly Miscellany*, Lyme Regis 1891–2; June 1891, ii. 58.

'The persons she created in *Persuasion,* Tennyson remarked as we were returning, were more real and living to him than Monmouth and his followers, whose landing-place on the western side of the Cobb we had just passed.'

    3. HALLAM TENNYSON, second Lord T. *Life* of his father 1897, ii. 47.

'On his arrival he called on Palgrave, and, refusing all refreshment, he said at once "Now take me to the Cobb, and show me the steps from which Louisa Musgrove fell".' See also 75, 105.

80. 1870. GOLDWIN SMITH. 'Jane Austen' in *The Nation,* New York 1870, x. 124.

'She has painted it [the society of English country gentlemen] as it was, in all its features, the most tragic as well as the most comic, avoiding only melodrama.'

81. 1870. AUSTEN-LEIGH: JAMES EDWARD, 1798–1874, only son of J. A.'s eldest brother James, became Austen-Leigh in

1837. His aunt died in 1817. *A Memoir of Jane Austen* by her nephew J. E. Austen-Leigh, Vicar of Bray, Berks. London, Richard Bentley, 1870.

Keynes 190. *Facts and Problems* 218. J. E. A.-L. in compiling his book relied on some of J. A.'s letters (he had not access to those published later by Lord Brabourne, see 95) and on his own recollections and those of his sister Caroline Austen and his (elder) half-sister Anna Lefroy. Some of their letters to him of information and advice have been preserved.

The *Memoir* is illustrated by an engraved portrait of J. A. by one Andrews of Maidenhead, based on a drawing by Cassandra (*Facts and Problems* 212; the original is now in the National Portrait Gallery; it had been reproduced in *Sailor Brothers* 1906, see 114), drawings by Anna Lefroy of Steventon Parsonage and Manor House and Chawton Church (but the parsonage had been demolished, and Mrs. Lefroy's drawing 'was made from *description* and is not perfectly correct'), and by a small facsimile of J. A.'s handwriting. See also 40, 43, 78, 82, 83, 119, and (p. 58) 78a.

82. 1871. J. E. AUSTEN-LEIGH. *A Memoir of Jane Austen*. By her nephew J. E. Austen-Leigh. Second Edition to which is added *Lady Susan* and fragments of two other unfinished tales by Miss Austen. London, Richard Bentley, 1871.

Keynes 191. *Facts and Problems* 218. In this edition, yielding to solicitation, J. E. A.-L. added some unpublished pieces of his aunt's work. This was against the judgement of Anna Lefroy, who would have tolerated publication of J. A.'s juvenile sketches, but was against publication of what she called 'betweenities'. The additions were (1) the cancelled chapter of *Persuasion* (29) (2) a description of 'The Last Work' —known to the family as *Sanditon*—with tantalizing extracts (30); (3) the fragment traditionally called *The Watsons* (26); (4) the short tale traditionally called *Lady Susan* (28). For later reprints of the *Memoir* see 83.

83. 1926. *Memoir*, &c. Edited by R. W. Chapman.

This edition has notes and index, and in its introduction an abridgement of the editor's article in *Times Lit. Suppt.* 14 Jan. 1926, which gave a full account of the collection, then recently dispersed, of J. A.'s MSS., &c., preserved in the family of her brother Admiral Charles John Austen. Part of this collection had been sold before I came to know its owners, and appeared at Sotheby's in 1948; see *Facts and Problems* 212. The text omits *Lady Susan* and *The Watsons*, since J. E. A.-L.'s texts had been superseded by R. W. C. in his separate editions printed from the autographs. My edition adds, to the illustrations from the edition of 1870 (mostly dropped in 1871), a fine portrait of J. E. A.-L.

84. 1870. *North British Review* lii, 1870, 129. Review of *Memoir*.

'Perhaps there is no author in existence in whom so marvellous a power of exhibiting characters . . . is combined with so total a want of the poetical imagination.' 'She expressly writes one of her novels . . . to show that the sudden passion is not the lasting affection.'

85. 1870. *Dublin Review* xv, N.S., 1870, 430. Review of *Memoir*.

Praise of the *Memoir* and rather lukewarm praise of its subject. The reviewer is shocked by J. A.'s worldly parsons. But, contradicting Scott, he finds Mr. Woodhouse and Miss Bates never tiresome. None of the novels has the quality of *The Vicar of Wakefield*. He notes that there are no caricatures except Robert Ferrars and Collins.

86. 1870. THOMAS EDWARD KEBBEL in *Fortnightly Review* xiii, 1870, 187. Review of *Memoir*.

'No trace' of Miss Mitford's 'love of nature'. J. A.'s concern is with 'minor mischiefs'.

87. 1870. *St. Paul's Magazine* v, 1870, 631. Review of *Memoir*.

   I had some hope of guessing this anonymous article to be by Trollope himself. But I do not think he would have put Steventon in Kent.

88. 1871. LADY RITCHIE (Anne Isabella Thackeray). Jane Austen in *Cornhill Magazine* xxiv, Aug. 1871, 158; reprinted in *Toilers and Spinsters*, Smith Elder 1874, 35–71; reprinted with (unimportant?) changes in *A Book of Sibyls* 1883.

   The essay is in effect a review of the *Memoir* of 1871. 'All these people nearly start out of the pages' (of J. A.'s novels).

89. 1878. LÉON BOUCHER in *Revue des Deux Mondes* xxix, 1878, 449. Review of 'Works 1872–77'.

   'Les romans de miss Austen sont au-dessus de semblables fluctuations (i.e. of fashion), non que tout y soit également admirable, mais parce qu'ils présentent dans leur ensemble quelques-uns de ces caractères qui assurent la durée aux œuvres classiques. A côté des richesses souvent trop éclatantes de l'imagination contemporaine, le talent de l'auteur de *Mansfield Park* paraît quelquefois un peu terne. On y voudrait plus de grâce, plus d'imprévu, quelque chose d'un peu plus féminin et d'un peu moins impersonnel. Il révèle néanmoins une femme supérieure dont on peut dire, en empruntant à Balzac le mot qu'il s'appliquait à lui-même, qu'elle a porté toute une société dans sa tête.'

90. 1882. RICHARD HOLT HUTTON. 'From Miss Austen to Mr. Trollope.' *Spectator* 55 (2), 1609.

   The writer deprecates 'the redness of the ink' used in Bentley's latest edition, as better suited to the speeches of Danton.
   'The change from Miss Austen to Mr. Trollope is the change from social home-rule to social centralisation' (i.e. in London) ... 'one prefers the home-rule'.

Biography and Criticism

91. 1882. *Saturday Review* 54, 23 Dec. 1882, 827. Review of the 'Steventon' edition of the novels.

'We have a dim remembrance of some one who wrote "The gelid critic prefers Miss Austen".'

92. 1882. ANNIE ARMITT. 'Jane Austen and Charlotte Brontë: a Contrast', in *Modern Review* iii, 1882, 384.

'No pilgrims wander to her grave as to a shrine; no curious literary studies can be made of her life or her character.' (Contrast the story of visitors to her grave in *Memoir* 1871, ch. vii.)

93. 1882. MARGARET OLIPHANT OLIPHANT. *Literary History of England* iii. 206.

'It would be difficult to find anything nearer witchcraft and magic.'

94. 1883. *Temple Bar* lxvii, 1883, 270. 'Is it Just? and a Bundle of Letters.'

R. Brimley Johnson, *Jane Austen* 1930, xi, very plausibly identified the author as Fanny Catherine Lefroy, a grand-daughter of James Austen.

The writer seeks to refute a recent critic, who had written 'Had Miss Austen felt more deeply, she would have written differently'.

'It is becoming the fashion to accuse her of being shallow and cold-hearted, and her heroines of being prudish.'

95. 1884. EDWARD KNATCHBULL-HUGESSEN, LORD BRABOURNE. *Letters of Jane Austen*, Bentley 1884, 2 vols. See 35.

The first Lord Brabourne was Edward Knatchbull (-Hugessen 1849), y. s. of Sir Edward Knatchbull of Provender, Kent, and Fanny Knight, J. A.'s niece. He inherited these letters from his mother. The MSS. were later dispersed, except those from J. A. to Fanny herself. The portrait-frontispiece (it was later cleaned, and in its cleaned state reproduced for the 1913 *Life*) is now believed to be probably not Zoffany and certainly not Jane Austen.

Facts and Problems 144.

96. 1884. Thomas W[illiam] Lyster in *Academy* xxvi, 1884, 333. Review of Brabourne's *Letters*.

'Only attend carefully, and see if you cannot piece together from successive keen scraps of characterisation a good notion of many of the people' (mentioned in her letters).

97. 1884. *Saturday Review* 58, 15 Nov. 1884, 637. Review of Brabourne's *Letters*.

The letters 'contain . . . the matter of the novels in solution—in a very diluted, and not always a very unmixed, solution—but still there'.

98. 1884. Richard Holt Hutton. *Spectator* 57 (2), 1482. Review of Brabourne's *Letters*.

The letters are 'far too full of domestic detail to be enjoyable'. Poor Lord Brabourne's 'own very dreary criticism' is castigated.

99. 1884. M. A. W. [Mary Augusta, Mrs. Humphrey Ward] in *Macmillan's Magazine* li, 1884, 84: 'Style and Miss Austen'.

A savage attack on Lord Brabourne for having done his great-aunt 'as ill a turn as it is in anybody's power to do to the author of *Pride and Prejudice*'.

'It was her possession of the qualities of condensation that made Jane Austen what she was. Condensation in literary matters means an exquisite power of choice and discrimination.'

100. 1884. *Athenaeum* 8 Nov. 1884, 585. Review of Brabourne's *Letters*.

The reviewer was bored by Lord B.'s family histories, and tempted to rank the interest of the letters themselves as only 'reliquarian'.

101. 1885. THOMAS EDWARD KEBBEL in *Fortnightly Review* xxxvii N.S. = xliii O.S., 1885 (1), 262. Review of Brabourne's *Letters*.

Praises Lord B.'s 'explanatory prefaces'. 'The pettiest and most commonplace details of domestic life may become amusing in the hands of this incomparable writer.'

102. 1885. SIR LESLIE STEPHEN. Jane Austen in *Dict. Nat. Biog.*

Brief and orthodox. Stephen dismissed the *Letters* of 1884 as 'trivial, and give no new facts'.

103. 1886. ANDREW LANG. *Letters to Dead Authors* 1886, 75–85.

'You are not a very popular author.'

104. 1889. JAMES ASHCROFT NOBLE in *Academy* xxxvi, 1889, 95, review of Mrs. Malden's *Jane Austen* (1889).

Mrs. M. is praised for 'sympathetic discrimination' but her method of 'summaries and samples' is condemned.

'Of Jane Austen herself this is not the place in which to speak. The remarkable and admirable qualities of her work have long been obvious . . . but we cannot help feeling conscious of a certain lack of weight which comes of her steady avoidance of the heights and the depths of human nature.'

105. 1890. ALFRED, LORD TENNYSON. *Memoirs by his Son* 1897, ii. 371.

'He would read and re-read . . . Miss Austen's novels. . . . The realism and life-likeness of Miss Austen's Dramatis Personae come nearest to those of Shakespeare. Shakespeare, however, is a sun to which Jane Austen, tho' a bright and true little world, is but an asteroid.' See also 75, 79.

1885–99

106. 1891. WALTER RALEIGH. *The English Novel.*

Defends J. A. against the stock complaints. 'The world of pathos and passion is present in her work by implication.' See however 124.

107. 1894. GEORGE SAINTSBURY. Preface to an edition of *Pride and Prejudice* published by George Allen 1894.

'If her knowledge was not very extended, she knew two things which only genius knows. The one was humanity and the other was art. On the first hand she could not make a mistake; her men, though limited, are true, and her women are, in the old sense, "absolute". As to art, if she has never tried idealism, her realism is real to a degree which makes the false realism of our own day look merely dead-alive. Take almost any Frenchman, except the late M. de Maupassant, and watch him laboriously piling up strokes in the hope of giving a complete impression. You get none. . . . But with Miss Austen the myriad, trivial, unforced strokes build up the picture like magic.'

108. 1894. ALICE MEYNELL. 'The Classic Novelist' in *Pall Mall Gazette* 16 Feb. 1894; reprinted in *The Second Person Singular* 1931.

'It is an unheavenly world.'

109. 1897. ADOLPHUS ALFRED JACK. *Essays on the Novel as Illustrated by Scott and Miss Austen* 1897, 232.

Quoting the encounter of Marianne with Willoughby in London, he comments: 'We seem here to catch a faint echo of those women who, springing from the pages of Bandello and Boccaccio, took form on the Elizabethan stage.' See 125.

110. 1899. WALTER HERRIES POLLOCK. *Jane Austen . . . an essay in criticism.*

Discriminating but orthodox praise.

Biography and Criticism

III. 1902. CONSTANCE HILL. *Jane Austen her Homes and her Friends.* Illustrations by Ellen G. Hill, 1902.

These ladies were pioneers. 'Armed with pen and pencil' they made their way in 'a country chaise' to Steventon, and thence followed their heroine to Reading, Bath, Lyme, Southampton, Stoneleigh, Chawton, Godmersham, and Winchester. They made the acquaintance of the various families and were shown manuscripts and portraits. The book is fully illustrated from authentic sources.

112. 1905. HENRY JAMES. *The Question of Our Speech, The Lesson of Balzac,* Boston and New York 1905, 60.

'Jane Austen, with all her light felicity, leaves us hardly more curious of her process, or of the experience in her that fed it, than the brown thrush who tells his story from the garden bough. . . . Practically over-looked for thirty or forty years after her death' [the tide of her reputation has now risen] 'rather higher . . . than the high-water mark . . . of her intrinsic interest. . . . Responsible, rather, is the body of publishers, editors, illustrators, producers of the present twaddle of magazines, who have found their "dear", our dear, everybody's dear, Jane so infinitely to their material purpose, so amenable to pretty reproduction in every variety of what is called tasteful, and in what seemingly proves to be saleable, form.

'I do not, naturally, mean that she would be saleable if we had not more or less—beginning with Macaulay, her first slightly ponderous amoroso—lost our hearts to her. . . .

'The key to Jane Austen's fortune with posterity has been in part the extraordinary grace of her facility, in part of her unconsciousness: as if, at the most, for difficulty, for embarrassment, she sometimes, over her work-basket, her tapestry flowers, in the spare, cool drawing-room of other days, fell a-musing, lapsed too metaphorically, as one may say, into wool-gathering, and her dropped stitches, of these pardonable, of these precious moments, were afterwards picked up as little touches of human truth, little glimpses of steady vision, little master-strokes of imagination.'

40

113. 1905. EDMUND CLERIHEW BENTLEY. *Biography for Beginners* 1905.

> The novels of Jane Austen
> Are the ones to get lost in.

114. 1906. JOHN H. and EDITH HUBBACK. *Jane Austen's Sailor Brothers*, John Lane 1906.

J. H. H. was a grandson of Sir Francis Austen; Edith, J. H. H.'s daughter. This book saw the first publication of J. A.'s letters to her brother Frank. It has a reproduction of Cassandra's drawing of her sister (see 81).

115. 1907. EDWARD VERRALL LUCAS. Introduction to *Emma* in World's Classics 1907.

'It would, I think, be found by any collector of the opinions of the best critics that *Emma* is considered to be Miss Austen's best novel.'

116. 1910. EDWARD VERRALL LUCAS in *Encyclopuedia Britannica*.

'She has become only lately a household word.' ·

117. 1911. ANDREW CECIL BRADLEY. Jane Austen, in *Essays and Studies* by Members of the English Association, vol. ii. Oxford 1911.

Facts and Problems 149, 170. 'Elaborate or technical criticism of her work begins with Bradley's essay.' This judgement perhaps does less than justice to some of the nineteenth-century critics.

118. 1911. *Chawton Manor and its Owners a Family History* by William Austen-Leigh . . . and Montagu George Knight.

Chawton Manor was inherited by J. A.'s brother Edward, who in 1812 took the name of Knight.

Biography and Criticism

119. 1911. MARY AUGUSTA AUSTEN-LEIGH. *James Edward Austen-Leigh a Memoir by his Daughter.* Privately printed 1911.

A life of J. A.'s nephew and biographer.

120. 1913. WILLIAM and RICHARD ARTHUR AUSTEN-LEIGH. *Jane Austen her Life and Letters a Family Record,* Smith Elder 1913 (two editions).

Facts and Problems 146, 167, where I risk calling this a definitive life. Although the emphasis is indicated by the sub-title, the *life* includes valuable critical comment; the *letters* are superseded by my fuller edition of 1932 (35).

121. 1913. GILBERT KEITH CHESTERTON. *The Victorian Age in Literature* 105, 109.

'No woman later has captured the complete common sense of Jane Austen. She could keep her head, while all the after women went about looking for their brains. . . .

Jane Austen was born before those bonds which (we are told) protected women from truth, were burst by the Brontës or elaborately untied by George Eliot. Yet . . . Jane Austen knew much more about men than either of them. Jane Austen may have been protected from truth: but it was precious little of truth that was protected from her.' This is illustrated from the character of Darcy.

122. 1915. HAROLD CHILD in *Cambridge Hist. of Eng. Lit.* XII. X. 244.

'. . . to attain, in the construction of her novels, as near as might be, to a perfection of form that should be the outcome of the interaction of the natures and motives in the story: these were her aims, and these aims she achieved, perhaps, with more consistency and more completeness than any other novelist except, it may be, de Maupassant.'

122*a*. 1915. LÉONIE VILLARD. *Jane Austen. Sa Vie et Son Œuvre*, Lyon 1915, 379 (a translation 1924).

'Il est un moment de l'aube où, dans la lumière fine et pâle du jour naissant, les lignes d'un paysage familier revêtent une apparence nouvelle. Sous la limpide clarté qui les baigne, elles prennent un caractère qu'on ne leur voit point aux heures illuminées d'un plus chaud rayonnement. Il semble alors que l'œil aperçoive pour la première fois ce décor, cependant bien connu, dont la magie de l'aube révèle un aspect jusque-là ignoré. Une même lueur, accompagnée d'une même révélation, éclaire l'œuvre de Jane Austen. . . . Une atmosphère de fraîcheur matinale, de sereine et pénétrante clarté, prête un intérêt inattendu à des êtres et des choses que rien n'élève au-dessus du niveau de la vie moyenne. L'auteur ne connaît et ne veut connaître que la douceur et la sécurité d'existences protégées contre toutes les surprises du destin; rien n'attire son attention ou n'excite sa curiosité qui ne s'épanouisse dans le climat intellectuel et social de la 'gentry'.

En dépit de ces restrictions, peut-être à cause d'elles, son roman traduit certains aspects du réel avec une lucidité et une justesse sans égales. Contradiction singulière . . . .'

123. 1917. REGINALD FARRER. 'Jane Austen', *Quarterly Review* 228, July 1917, 7, 20, 25.

'Readers fall into two groups—the objective and the subjective. And it is only the objective class who, because emotion is not vehemently expressed by Jane Austen, will fail to realise with what profound effect it is implied. . . .'

' "Mansfield Park" is vitiated throughout by a radical dishonesty. . . .'

'While twelve readings of "Pride and Prejudice" give you twelve periods of pleasure repeated, as many readings of "Emma" give you that pleasure, not repeated only, but squared and squared again with each perusal, till at every fresh reading you feel anew that you never understood anything like the widening sum of its delights.'

124. 1917. SIR WALTER RALEIGH. *Letters 1879–1922* 1926.

Letter 23 Oct. 1917 to R. W. C., condemning J. A.'s young men. *Facts and Problems* 224. See also 106.

125. 1919. GEORGE MOORE in *Avowals* 1919.

Of *S. and S.*: 'It is here [Marianne's meeting with Willoughby in London] that we find the burning human heart in English prose narrative for the first and, alas, for the last time' (p. 40 in the 1924 edition).

126. 1920. MARY AUGUSTA AUSTEN-LEIGH (daughter of J. E. A.-L.). *Personal Aspects of Jane Austen* 1920.

An appendix quotes recollections of life at Chawton written in 1867 by J. E. A.-L.'s sister Caroline. See also 78*a*, p. 57.

127. 1922. ROBERT WILLIAM CHAPMAN. 'Jane Austen's Methods', *Times Lit. Suppt.* 9 Feb. 1922.

I believe I was the first to suggest that the method of *Emma* is a fore-runner of the method of Henry James. See 168.

128. 1923. VIRGINIA WOOLF. 'Jane Austen at Sixty', *Nation* 15 Dec. 1923, xxxiv. 433, expanded as 'Jane Austen' in *The Common Reader*, Hogarth Press 1925.

Facts and Problems 171. The golden sentence—'Of all great writers she is the most difficult to catch in the act of greatness'—is in the review but was (unhappily?) dropped from the final essay.

'She would (if she had lived) have been the forerunner of Henry James and Proust.' See 130.

See also, in *The Common Reader*, remarks on Emma Woodhouse at the ball (43, repeated 216), and on Emma Watson, also at a ball (301).

129. 1923. MARJORY A. BALD. *Women Writers of the Nineteenth Century*, Cambridge 1923, 1–27.

'In the midst of a period restless, curious, and impassioned, she preserved her faith in moderation and discipline. . . . Without obtrusive effort or exertion of visible influence she gave to her world what it most required—an example of reserved and ordered serenity.'

130. 1924. RUDYARD KIPLING. *The Janeites* in *The Story-Teller*, May 1924. Reprinted in *Debits and Credits* 1926.

The drunken mess-waiter is quoted: 'Pa-hardon me, gents, but this *is* a matter on which I *do* 'appen to be moderately well-informed. She *did* leave lawful issue in the shape o' one son; an' 'is name was 'Enery James.'

Facts and Problems 204. Did Kipling allude to the dramatic method of *Emma*? See 127, 128, 168.

131. 1924. EDWARD MORGAN FORSTER. Review of R. W. C.'s edition of the novels, *Nation* 5 Jan. 1924, xxxiv. 512: 'Jane, how shall we ever recollect?' (quoting one of Miss Bates's speeches at the Crown). Reprinted, as 'Jane Austen. 1. The Six Novels' in *Abinger Harvest* 1936.

'Yet with all the help in the world how shall we drag these shy, proud books into the centre of our minds? To be one with Jane Austen! It is a contradiction in terms, yet every Jane Austenite has made the attempt. When the humour has been absorbed and the cynicism and moral earnestness discounted, something remains which is easily called Life, but does not thus become more approachable.' See also 132, 151.

132. 1925. EDWARD MORGAN FORSTER. Review of *Sanditon*, *Nation* xxxvi, 860. 21 Mar. 1925. Reprinted as 'Jane Austen. 2. Sanditon' in *Abinger Harvest* 1936. *Facts and Problems* 171.

'. . . not only does the sea dance in freshness, but another configuration has been given to the earth, making it at once more poetic and more definite. Sanditon gives out an atmosphere, and also exists as a geographic and economic force. . . . The change is merely interesting because it took place in her mind—that self-contained mind which had hitherto regarded the face of the earth as a site for shrubberies and strawberry beds, and had denied it features of its own.' See also 131, 151.

133. 1925. ANNETTE B[ROWN] HOPKINS. 'Jane Austen, the Critic', *Publication of the Modern Language Association of America* June 1925, xl. 398.

An exhaustive account of J. A.'s reading and her opinions on the books she read.

134. 1926. LORD GERALD WELLESLEY (now Duke of Wellington). 'Houses in Jane Austen's Novels', *Spectator* 20 Mar. 1926, cxxxvi. 524.

135. 1928. HEATHCOTE WILLIAM GARROD. 'Jane Austen, a Depreciation', in *Essays by Divers Hands* (R. Society of Literature) 1928.

'Written without thought of publication, for a pleasant occasion, and in lightness of heart.' See 147 for an attempt at refutation.

136. 1928. JAMES DESMOND MACCARTHY (later Sir Desmond). 'Unity and Effect' in *New Statesman* 8 Sept. 1928, reprinted in *Criticism* 1932, 232.

'. . . the fatal flaw in Henry James's theory. If the narrator is abolished, the characters who narrate in his place become inevitably endowed with the novelist's own peculiar faculties and intellectual temper.'

Must we then equate Emma with her creator? See 127.

137. 1928. EDWIN MUIR. *The Structure of the Novel* 1928, ii. 42–45.

Mr. Muir discusses *P. and P.* as a 'dramatic novel', distinguished from the 'novel of action and character'. J. A. is 'the first novelist who practised it with consummate success in England.' See also 170.

138. 1929. MARY LASCELLES. Introduction to *Mansfield Park* in World's Classics 1929.

'*Facts and Problems* 223. See also 160*a*.

139. 1929. ROBERT WILLIAM CHAPMAN. Introduction to *Pride and Prejudice* in World's Classics 1929.

140. 1929. LADY BALFOUR (widow of Sir Graham B.). 'The Servants in Jane Austen', *Cornhill Magazine* Dec. 1929, N.S. lxvii. 697.

141. 1929. C[LARA] LINKLATER THOMSON, *Jane Austen a Survey* 1929.

Facts and Problems 224.

142. 1930. MICHAEL SADLEIR. Introduction to *Northanger Abbey* in World's Classics 1930.

A discussion of the 'horrid' novels. Mr. Sadleir suggests that Crosbie's decision not to publish *Susan* may have had a commercial motive. Himself a publisher of Gothic romances, he might think that a book ridiculing them would be a failure and might even be damaging.

143. 1930. ROBERT WILLIAM CHAPMAN. 'Jane Austen and her Publishers', *London Mercury* Aug. 1930, xxii. 337.

Collects the evidence for the publishing and financial history of the novels up to the acquisition of the copyrights by Bentley.

144. 1930. CHARLES BEECHER HOGAN. 'Sir Walter Scott and *Emma*', *PMLA*, Dec. 1930, xlv. 1267.

Scott's authorship of the *Quarterly Review* of *E.* (46) had been questioned; it was here established.

145. 1930. FORREST REID. Introduction to *Persuasion* in World's Classics 1930.

'Jane Austen had no gift for treating an adventure (even one so domestic as poor Louisa's), she had no gift for poetry, no sense of mystery, no knowledge of the heights and depths of passion, and if she had a more than superficial feeling for nature she kept it severely under restraint...

'The delicate love reveries of Anne Elliot possess a perennial freshness; the colour has not faded nor the salt lost its savour. There is no strangeness in *Persuasion*, there are no surprises. . . . But there is a mind in it, tenderness, humour, irony, the charm of a delightful personality, and above all there is life.'

146. 1931. JOHN CANN BAILEY. *Introductions to Jane Austen* 1931.

A reprint of his introductions to the Georgian Edition (Eveleigh Nash 1927) of the six novels and of *Lady Susan* and *The Watsons*; to which B. added an essay on *Love and Freindship* and *Sanditon*.

Facts and Problems 173, 195, where I confess that I had found Bailey's attitude pontifical. A sympathetic review (*Times Lit. Suppt.* 12 Nov. 1931, by Mr. Percy Lubbock, as I learned on authority) after describing J. A.'s world with admiration, poses the question 'what is she to set these men and women to *do*?' and states the answer in terms of walks, picnics, chills and sprained ankles—and how much she makes of them! Had Mr. Lubbock forgotten that J. A.'s people, however socially or geographically circumscribed, had to meet the strains of family life, and to fall in love, with the right or wrong person; that the moral and emotional problems of being in love are indeed J. A.'s main preoccupation?

147. 1931. ROBERT WILLIAM CHAPMAN. 'Jane Austen: A Reply to Mr. Garrod'. In *Essays by Divers Hands* (R. Society of Literature), Oxford University Press 1931. See 135.

148. 1931. SIR FRANK DOUGLAS MACKINNON. In *Times Lit. Suppt.* 10 and 31 Dec. 1931.

Attempt to identify Mansfield Park with Cottesbrooke in Northamptonshire, the seat of Sir James Langham, Bart., at the date of *M.P.* See for corroboration above, 6; and for an account of Cottesbrooke, *Country Life* 15 February 1936.

149. 1931. LORD DAVID CECIL. Introduction to *Sense and Sensibility* in World's Classics 1931. See 155.

'The visible structure of Jane Austen's stories may be flimsy enough; but their foundations drive deep down into the basic principles of human conduct. On her bit of ivory she has engraved a criticism of life as serious and as considered as Hardy's.'

150. 1932. ROBERT WILLIAM CHAPMAN. Introduction to his edition of the *Letters*. See 35.

151. 1932. EDWARD MORGAN FORSTER. Review of R. W. C.'s edition of the *Letters*, *Times Lit. Suppt.* 10 Nov. 1932: 'Miss Austen and Jane Austen'. Reprinted, as 'Jane Austen. 3. The Letters' in *Abinger Harvest* 1936.

Facts and Problems 106. Mr. Forster invites his readers to walk in the rectory garden and to guess what is wrong: 'Can it be the drains?' In one passage he hears 'the whinnying of harpies'. See also 131, 132.

152. 1932. HUGH DE SELINCOURT. 'Incomparable Jane Austen', review, *Everyman* 19 Nov. 1932, of *Letters* 1932 (35).

'Some people by their wit are able to lend a sort of grace to the dreariest little affairs of daily life. . . . Their graciousness can transform what is apt to become a necessary nuisance into something quite different . . . by facing the fact of the necessary nuisance and somehow infecting it with their laughing. It is a rare gift, and a very lovely one, and these letters showed Jane Austen possessed it in all its plenitude.'

153. 1932. HON. (now Sir) HAROLD NICOLSON. *New Statesman and Nation* 26 Nov. 1932. Review of *Letters* 1932 (35).

The reader 'settles down to enjoy himself. And once again comes over him that feeling of perplexed disappointment. It is not merely that Jane Austen's letters to her sister Cassandra are trivial and dull. It is far worse than that. Inevitably, as we plough through this desert of family gossip, this catalogue of sun-bonnets, the ghastly thought arises that Jane Austen had a mind like a very small, sharp pair of scissors, attached by a pink ribbon to a very neat and maidenly work-basket.'

Facts and Problems 224.

154. 1933. ROBERT WILLIAM CHAPMAN. 'Jane Austen's Library', *Book Collectors' Quarterly* xi, July–Sept. 1933, 28.

This article supplements Keynes 367–71. I can now add that Goldsmith's *History* belongs to Mr. R. A. Austen-Leigh, that Hume's is at Yale, that Hayley's *Poems and Plays* has been resumed by a member of J. A.'s family, and that Thomson's *Works* 1773 belonged to Virginia Woolf, who had also, in 1936, J. A.'s Ariosto (but threatened to give it away). Elkin Mathews in 1945 offered (Cat. 100, 2) Isaac Disraeli's *Curiosities of Literature* 1791, with J. A.'s signature on the title-page. Mr. W. R. Batty has *Bell's Travels* 1764, with J. A.'s autograph and the date 1799. See also p. 58.

155. 1935. LORD DAVID CECIL. *Jane Austen: the Leslie Stephen Lecture* 1935. See 149.

Facts and Problems 222. Reviewed (R. W. C.) in *Time and Tide* 27 July 1935.

'On her own ground Jane Austen gets to the heart of the matter; her graceful unpretentious philosophy, founded as it is on an unwavering recognition of fact, directed by an unerring perception of moral quality, is as impressive as those of the most majestic novelists. Myself I find it more impressive. If I were in doubt as to the wisdom of one of my actions I should not consult Flaubert or Dostoievsky. The opinion of Balzac or Dickens would carry little weight with me: were Stendhal to rebuke me, it would only convince me I had done right: even in the judgment of Tolstoy I should not put complete confidence. But I should be seriously upset, I should worry for weeks and weeks, if I incurred the disapproval of Jane Austen.'

156. 1936. ELIZABETH BOWEN. 'Jane Austen: Artist on Ivory'
(but Miss Bowen told me that the last three words were due to
the editor), *Saturday Review of Literature* 15 Aug. 1936.

Facts and Problems 172, where I venture the opinion that the essay
is 'full of striking, if often disputable, judgements'.

'Returning again and again to Mr. Darcy, one pays Jane Austen the
compliment of deciding that there was more to him than she knew. He
has that cloudy outline important characters should have; does not seem
to have been "created" in the limited brainbound sense so much as observed fleetingly out of the corner of an eye, recollected uncertainly,
speculated upon. One takes him to be a devious, constantly self-regard-
ing, and very passionate man—but he soars out of the picture—most of
him happens off. In a woman writer's book, any man who is intended
to be either important or magnetic ought to have this quality.'

157. 1937. EMMA AUSTEN-LEIGH. *Jane Austen and Steventon*
1937.

158. 1938. MONA WILSON. *Jane Austen and Some Contem-
poraries* 1938, 6.

'I can never make up my mind whether Miss Austen knows what an
odious woman Elinor is, or whether she is the one failure.'

159. 1938. ELIZABETH JENKINS. *Jane Austen, a Biography*,
Gollancz 1938. Reprinted 1948.

The Introduction to this accurate and understanding book modestly
claims that it is the only strictly chronological life. *Facts and
Problems* 174.

160. 1939. EMMA AUSTEN-LEIGH. *Jane Austen and Bath*
1939.

160a. 1939. MARY LASCELLES. *Jane Austen and her Art.*

Facts and Problems 174. This subtle piece of analysis is closely woven,
and brief quotation would hardly be representative. See also 138.

163614

Biography and Criticism

161. 1940. [RICHARD ARTHUR AUSTEN-LEIGH]. *Pedigree of Austen*, privately printed 1940.

Begins, tentatively, with a William Astyn of Yalding in Kent, whose will was proved 1522 and (in my copy, with corrections and additions by the author) comes down to 1940.

162. 1940–52. DENYS WYATT HARDING. 'Regulated Hatred: An Aspect of the Work of Jane Austen', *Scrutiny* viii, Mar. 1940, 346.—REUBEN A. BROWER. 'The Controlling Hand: Jane Austen and *Pride and Prejudice*', *Scrutiny* xiii, Sept. 1945, 99.—MARVIN MUDRICK. *Jane Austen: Irony as Defense and Discovery*, Princeton University Press 1952.

I group these essays in iconoclasm (they are grouped in Mr. Mudrick's preface) as seeming to issue from a common view, and that one with which I am so out of sympathy that I do not trust myself to discriminate. 'Jane Austen's compulsion, and genius, is to look only for incongruity.' So Mr. Mudrick, who finds J. A., novelist or letter-writer, as hard-boiled as her Emma, whose dominant quality is her want of tenderness. He quotes, as a motto, this from Mr. Harding: 'her books are, as she meant them to be, read and enjoyed by precisely the sort of people whom she disliked; she is a literary classic of the society which opinions like hers, held widely enough, would undermine', and himself holds (p. vii) that *Emma* is a novel admired, even consecrated, for qualities which it in fact subverts or ignores'. (He does not discuss the Opinions of *M.P.* and *E.* that J. A. was at pains to collect; see 33.) Reviews by R. W. C. in *T.L.S.* 19.9.1952, W. Husbands in *R.E.S.*, July 1954.

163. 1941–2. Q[UEENIE] D[OROTHY] LEAVIS. 'A Critical Theory of Jane Austen's Writings'; 'II. *Lady Susan* into *Mansfield Park*', *Scrutiny* x. 61, 114, 272, June and Oct. 1941, Jan. 1942.

Quotation might I fear do less than justice to this ingenious and elaborate construction. I am unable to accept the identification of Mary Crawford with J. A.'s cousin and sister-in-law Eliza, on which the argument largely hinges. (*Facts and Problems* 127; I wrote not knowing that Mrs. Leavis had given her authority to this doctrine.)

164. 1942. RICHARD ARTHUR AUSTEN-LEIGH. *Austen Papers 1704–1856.* Privately printed by Spottiswoode Ballantyne & Co. 1942.

Family history, with many references to J. A. and one letter to her from her cousin Edward Cooper.

165. 1944. EDMUND WILSON in *The New Yorker* 24 June 1944.

Jane Austen is 'unique among the novelists of her sex in being . . . concerned, not with the vicarious satisfaction of emotion . . . but, as the great masculine novelists are, with the novel as a work of art'.

166. 1947. SAMUEL KLIGER. 'Jane Austen's *Pride and Prejudice* in the Eighteenth-Century Mode', *University of Toronto Quarterly* xvi. 357, July 1947.

An analysis of *P. and P.* as an 'art-nature' study in terms of eighteenth-century 'neo-classical' literary theory. The essay is polysyllabic, and open to the familiar objection that its subject would not have understood it; for J. A. might turn in her grave if informed of her 'carefully premeditated plan for increasing the availability of the art-nature antithesis for the love plot or basic situation of the novel'. The study is none the less ponderable: an example of the philosophical approach to literary criticism now so characteristic of American scholarship.

167. 1948. SAMUEL C. CHEW. *A Literary History of England,* Appleton-Century–Crofts 1948, 1200–6.

168. 1948. FRANK RAYMOND LEAVIS. *The Great Tradition: George Eliot, Henry James, Joseph Conrad,* 7, 10.

Though Mr. Leavis's main theme is the three writers of his title, he prefixes J. A. in his first chapter as one of our four great novelists.

(Dickens is admitted, but only in virtue of *Hard Times*.) It is the more disappointing that his treatment of J. A. is brief.

'The principle of organization . . . in her work is an intense moral interest of her own in life that is in the first place a preoccupation with certain problems that life compels on her as personal ones. . . . Without her intense moral preoccupation she couldn't have been a great novelist.'

Henry James 'can't have failed to note with interest that *Emma* fulfils, by anticipation, a prescription of his own: everything is presented through Emma's dramatized consciousness'. See 127.

169. 1948. ROBERT WILLIAM CHAPMAN. *Jane Austen, Facts and Problems.* The Clark Lectures at Trinity College, Cambridge 1948. Oxford 1948; third edition, with a few corrections 1950.

I have thought it permissible to refer frequently in these pages to my modest compendium, as the only book that attempts to assemble all the evidence, at least by reference. The *Times* reviewer (26 Feb 1949) suggested, most gently, that perhaps I had 'taken her more seriously than she would have taken herself'. The obvious answer, I think, is *Mansfield Park.*

170. 1949. EDWIN MUIR. 'Jane Austen and the Sense of Evil', *New York Times Book Review* 28 Aug. 1949.

'The action is confined to people living according to a set code of manners. Personal relations in accordance with that code are all that remain, are the sole subject of study. Jane Austen is the first English novelist who devoted her genius to that theme. She is the real forerunner of Henry James and Virginia Woolf and E. M. Forster and Ivy Compton-Burnett.' See also 137.

171. 1950. JOYCE MARJORIE SANXTER TOMPKINS. Review of R. W. C.'s *Facts and Problems, Review of English Studies* N.S. i. 4, Oct. 1950.

I include this notice, however flattering to its subject, because it struck me as outstandingly perceptive.

172. 1950. ROBERT WILLIAM CHAPMAN. Jane Austen, in *Chambers's Encyclopaedia.*

173. 1950. MARGARET KENNEDY. *Jane Austen* 83.

'It is the ambient air of Highbury which most charms us in this book. The little town and all its inhabitants are so real, so actual, that it is hard to believe we have never been there. The very cobbles, glistening after a sharp shower, are nearly solid enough to walk on. The sun burns our necks over Mr. Knightly's strawberry beds and the shade in Donwell Lane is refreshing. It is as if that stretching of imagination, which enabled Miss Austen to like Emma, gave her a firmer grasp upon everything within reach.'

This writer's distinction, and her popularity, as a novelist will compel attention to her critical judgements. She has thought much, and to good effect, on the novelist's art. But her account of the 'background' (chap. I), though it has much that is justly and acutely seen, is I think slightly but fatally distorted. The account of J. A.'s specific environment is in some respects gravely misleading. Many eyes will open wide in surprise to read that 'her existence was spent on a sofa beside people like old Mrs. Musgrove'.

174. 1950. LOUIS KRONENBERGER. Introduction to *Pride and Prejudice,* Harper.

'With the merest trifle Jane Austen can exert great force and intensity. Emma's rudeness to Miss Bates at a picnic becomes as dramatic as a lesser novelist's buffalo stampede; evokes as sharp a moral crisis as the temptation, in a lesser novel, to betray one's country.'

175. 1952. CHARLES BEECHER HOGAN. 'Jane Austen and her Early Public' in *Review of English Studies* N.S. i. 4, Oct. 1950, 39.

An examination of early reviews of the novels, valuable as showing their impact on the contemporary public.

176. 1952. EDD WINFIELD PARKS. 'Exegesis in Austen's Novels', *South Atlantic Quarterly* li. 1, Jan. 1952.

'The author does not allow the reader to see the whole character immediately. We see instead only as much . . . as the main person—in every case the heroine—sees and comprehends. . . .'

'When, like Catherine Morland, the heroine is too immature or, like Fanny Price, too weak to assume the full burden of central intelligence, Miss Austen is frequently the exegete' (whereas Elizabeth, Emma, and Anne do most of the work for her).

177. 1952. MARGARET KENNEDY. 'How ought a Novelist . . . ?', *Fortnightly Review* Nov. 1952.

'George Eliot is obviously upon the defensive lest we should think Dorothea a prig and a bluestocking; she is frequently at the elbow of the reader to remind him of the handicaps and limitations with which the poor girl has to contend. Miss Austen, on the other hand, allows Fanny to use the stilted language of contemporary books on the picturesque without comment, and without reminding us that such books were Fanny's only guides when she wished to express a very genuine enjoyment of natural beauty. When Fanny declares that she loves to look at "verdure", it is left to the reader to remember that she probably does not know what else to call it, that she lives among people who seldom call it anything and seldom look at it. . . .

'Some readers do call Fanny a prig. Some readers can never forgive Emma for her lapse of manners on Box Hill. But Miss Austen gains far more than she loses by this grand casualness which leaves so much to the reader, whether she is writing of Elizabeth Bennet, whom she expects to capture every heart, or of Emma Woodhouse, whom she expects nobody to like much save herself. For this casualness springs from a supreme confidence which took her at one bound óver a fence from which nearly all other novelists, even the greatest, have been obliged to turn aside.'

178. 1952. (Sir) WINSTON S. CHURCHILL. *The Second World War* v. 377.

'I decided to read a novel. I had long ago read Jane Austen's *Sense and*

Sensibility, and now I thought I would have *Pride and Prejudice*. Sarah read it to me beautifully from the foot of the bed. I had always thought it would be better than its rival. What calm lives they had, those people! No worries about the French Revolution, or the crashing struggle of the Napoleonic wars. Only manners controlling natural passion so far as they could, together with cultured explanations of any mischances. All this seemed to go very well with M and B.'

ADDENDA

13. I strangely forgot Routledge's Sixpenny Novels; strangely, because I possess Housman's copies of *S and S* and *P and P* (but he did no more than correct misprints). Messrs. Routledge inform me that they published all the novels in this series in 1883. I am credibly informed that they could be obtained not for sixpence only, but also for a certain number of soap-wrappers. The paper covers have an illustration in front, on the back an advertisement of Pears' Soap, with what are now called endorsements by Mme Patti, Mrs. Langtry, Mary Anderson, and others.

42. I ought to have seen that 1814 is impossible for 'Scott's novels'. Miss Winifred Husbands tells me that Herries visited Montreal only in Lord Amherst's absence, 1823–28.

57*a*. 1838. HARRIETT ELIZABETH MOZLEY, Newman's sister, in a letter of 2 Nov. 1838 (*T.L.S.* 17 Sept. 1954) describes a visit to the Fowle family and reports Mr. Fowle's account of J. A. He was Fulwar William, 1791–1876. His mother Eliza, née Lloyd, was sister of Mrs. James Austen and of Martha Lloyd. J. A. in 1805 (Letter 44) writes of his 'attentive, affectionate feelings'.

'He gave a very nice and satisfactory account of her—he said she was pretty—certainly pretty—bright and a good deal of color in her face—like a doll—no that would not give at all the idea for she had so much expression—she was like a child—

quite a child very lively and full of humor—most amiable—
most beloved—he says the Austins are all clever—clever in a
way—they write verses etc. rather elegantly and are agreeable
—but not superior—that Jane and James were far above the
others and were truly superior—the others had much vanity—
there was not a glimpse about those two'.—Readers of J. A'.s
letters will form their own opinion on the matters of superiority
and vanity.

78a. 1867. CAROLINE MARY CRAVEN AUSTEN, 1805–80. *My
Aunt Jane Austen.* Printed for Jane Austen Soc. 1952. See 126.

A little gem of sympathetic and perceptive reminiscence.

154. Mr. Munby tells me that Mrs. Woolf *did* give away
J. A.'s copy of Hoole's *Ariosto* 1783 (5 volumes); she gave it to
Maynard (later Lord) Keynes. It is in King's College Library.

179. 1953. LIONEL TRILLING. *A Portrait of Western Man.
The Listener* 11 June 1953, 969.

Mr. Trilling in an essay that will doubtless be reprinted makes a
distinction between Character and Personality, exploring the theme
by consideration of J. A., Dickens, and D. H. Lawrence. He sees in
J. A. the first novelist to study the play and development of personality.

Mr. Trilling resents the moral and religious orthodoxy of *Mansfield Park*, and his view of the society depicted in the novels is shown
by my quotation:—

'Jane Austen was conscious of, or unconsciously aware of, not a
good society but a bad one, a predominately vulgar society, which
was, nevertheless, the field in which spirit discovered and developed
its own nature.'

180. 1954. ELIZABETH BOWEN. 'What Jane Austen Means to
Me', *Everybody's* 15 May 1954.

Miss Bowen's perceptive analysis might have been entitled 'The
Novelist's Novelist'.

INDEX

Index

Index

Forster, Edward Morgan, 131 (the novels), 132 (Sanditon), 151 (the letters).
Fortnightly Review, 101 (Kebbel).
Fox, Henry Stephen (1791–1846), 44.
Fraser's Magazine, 63 (Lewes), 74 (Fitzgerald).

Garrod, Heathcote William, 135.

Harding, Denys W., 162.
Hill, Constance, 111.
Hogan, Charles Beecher, 144, 175.
Hopkins, Annette Brown, 133.
Howard, George William Frederick, Viscount Morpeth (1802–64), 56.
Hubback, John H. and Edith, 114.

Jack, Adolphus Alfred (1868–1946), 109.
James, Henry (1843–1916), 112.
Jenkins, Elizabeth, 159.

Kavanagh, Julia, 76.
Kebbel, Thomas Edward, 86, 101.
Kennedy, Margaret, 173, 177.
Kipling, Rudyard (1865–1936), 130.
Kirk, John Foster, 69.
Kliger, Samuel, 166.
Knatchbull-Hugessen, Edward, Lord Brabourne (1829–93), 95–101.
Knight, Montagu George, 118.
Kronenberger, Louis, 174.

Lang, Andrew (1844–1912), 103.
Lascelles, Mary, 138, 160a.
Leavis, Frank Raymond, 168.
Leavis, Queenie Dorothy, 163.
Lefroy, Fanny Catherine, 94.
Lewes, George Henry (1817–78), 63, 65, 67, 72.
Lubbock, Percy, 146.

Lucas, Edward Verrall (1868–1938), 115, 116.
Lyster, Thomas William, 84.

Macaulay, Thomas Babington, Lord M. (1800–59), 62, 70.
MacCarthy, Sir James Desmond (1877–1952), 136.
MacKinnon, Sir Frank Douglas (1871–1946), 148.
Mackintosh, Sir James (1765–1832), 52.
Macmillan's Magazine, 99 (Ward).
Meynell, Alice Christiana Gertrude (1847–1922), 108.
Mitford, Mary Russell (1787–1855), 45, 68.
Modern Language Association of America, 133 (Hopkins).
Modern Review, 92 (Armitt).
Moore, George (1852–1933), 125.
Morpeth, *see* Howard.
Mozley, James Bowling (1813–78), 58.
Mudrick, Marvin, 162.
Muir, Edwin, 137, 170.

Nation, The (London), 131, 132 (Forster).
Nation, The (New York), 80 (Goldwin Smith).
Newman, John Henry (1801–90), 57.
New Statesman and Nation, 153 (Nicolson).
New Yorker, The, 165.
Nicolson, Hon. Sir Harold, 153.
Noble, James Ashcroft, 104.
North American Review, 69 (Kirk).
North British Review, 84.

Oliphant, Oliphant Margaret (1828–97), 93.

61

Index

PRINTED IN
GREAT BRITAIN
AT THE
UNIVERSITY PRESS
OXFORD
BY
CHARLES BATEY
PRINTER
TO THE
UNIVERSITY

Date Due